Copyright and Legal Disclaimer

Copyright ©2024 by Morgan Clickson. All rights reserved.

No part of this publication may be reproduced, distributed, or transmitted in any form or by any means, including photocopying, recording, or other electronic or mechanical methods, without the prior written permission of the publisher, except in the case of brief quotations embodied in critical reviews and certain other noncommercial uses permitted by copyright law.

The advice and strategies contained herein may not be suitable for your situation. You should consult with a professional where appropriate. The publisher is not engaged in rendering legal, accounting, or other professional services. If legal advice or other expert assistance is required, the services of a competent professional should be sought.

The publisher and the author make no representations or warranties with respect to the accuracy or completeness of the contents of this book and specifically disclaim all warranties, including without limitation warranties of fitness for a particular purpose. No warranty may be created or extended by sales representatives or written sales materials. The advice and strategies contained herein may not be suitable for every situation. Neither the publisher nor the author shall be liable for damages arising herefrom.

The fact that an organization or website is referred to in this work as a citation and/or a potential source of further information does not mean that the author or the publisher endorses the information the organization or website may provide or recommendations it may make. Further, readers should be aware that internet websites listed in this work may have changed or disappeared between when this work was written and when it is read.

Trademarks: All brand names and product names used in this book are trade names, service marks, trademarks, or registered trademarks of their respective owners. The publisher is not associated with any product or vendor mentioned in this book.

Note to the Reader:

This publication is designed to provide accurate and authoritative information in regard to the subject matter covered. It is sold with the understanding that the publisher and the author are not liable for the misconception or misuse of information provided. The information provided in this book is meant for educational and entertainment purposes only. This book does not constitute financial, legal, or professional advice. Any action taken upon the information on this book is strictly at your own risk, and the author will not be liable for any losses and damages in connection with the use of this book.

Contents

Understanding the Basics of Digital Advertising 6
    Key Terms and Concepts in Digital Advertising 7
Optimizing Your Search Engine for Best Traffic 10
    Understanding Search Engine Optimization (SEO) 10
    Keyword Research and Analysis for SEO 11
Leveraging Targeted Ads on Social Media Platforms 14
    Choosing the Right Social Media Platforms for Your Business 14
    Creating Targeted Ads for Different Audience Segments 15
    Analyzing and Adjusting Social Media Ad Campaigns for Maximum ROI 17
Maximizing Visibility with Google AdWords Campaigns 18
    Optimizing Ad Copy and Keywords for Better Performance 20
Increasing Conversions with Retargeting Ads 22
    Understanding Retargeting and Its Benefits 22
    Creating Effective Retargeting Campaigns 24
    Analyzing Retargeting Data to Improve Conversions 25
Creating Compelling Ad Copy and Landing Pages 26
    Writing Engaging Ad Copy that Drives Clicks 26
    Designing Landing Pages for Better User Engagement 28
    Testing and Optimizing Ad Copy and Landing Pages for Conversions 29
Tracking and Analyzing Digital Advertising Data 31
    Importance of Data Tracking and Analysis in Digital Advertising .. 31
    Tools and Techniques for Analyzing Advertising Data 32

Making Informed Decisions Based on Data Insights 34
A/B Testing for Optimal Performance..35
    Understanding A/B Testing and Its Benefits 35
    Implementing A/B Tests for Ads and Landing Pages 37
    Interpreting Results and Making Data-Driven Decisions 38
Integrating Digital Advertising and SEO Efforts.................................40
    Importance of Aligning Digital Advertising and SEO Strategies 40
    Creating a Cohesive Marketing Strategy.....................................41
    Maximizing Results by Combining Digital Advertising and SEO Tactics. 42
Navigating the Future with Emerging Digital Advertising Platforms ..44
    TikTok: Unleashing Creative Potential..44
    Pinterest: Pinning Your Way to Visibility.....................................44
    Snapchat: Capturing Moments, Capturing Audiences.................45
    Navigating the New Frontier 45
Mastering Video Advertising Techniques for Small Business Success 46
    Crafting Compelling Video Content 46
    Optimizing Video for Different Platforms....................................47
    Leveraging Video SEO 48
    Measuring Success and Iteration 48
    Conclusion: The Power of Video Advertising...............................48
Harnessing the Power of Influencer Marketing 49
    Understanding Influencer Marketing...49
    Identifying the Right Influencers 50
    Crafting Your Influencer Marketing Strategy...............................50

- Navigating Influencer Collaborations 51
- Measuring Success 51
- Building Success with Influencer Marketing 52

Navigating Privacy Regulations and Data Protection in Digital Advertising.. 52
- The Importance of Privacy and Data Protection 52
- Understanding Key Privacy Regulations 53
- Implementing Data Protection Practices....................................... 53
- Handling Data Breaches 54
- Building Trust Through Compliance 54

Leveraging Advanced Analytics and AI for Strategic Digital Advertising.. 55
- The Power of Advanced Analytics 55
- AI-Driven Advertising 56
- Tools to Enhance Your Advertising Efforts 56
- Implementing AI and Advanced Analytics in Your Strategy........... 56
- Navigating the Future of Digital Advertising................................. 57

Mastering Interactive and Immersive Ads for Engaging Digital Experiences... 58
- The Rise of Interactive and Immersive Advertising 58
- Benefits of Interactive and Immersive Ads 58
- Implementing Interactive and Immersive Ads.............................. 59
- Tools and Platforms for Creating Interactive and Immersive Ads..60
- Crafting the Future of Advertising 60

Understanding the Basics of Digital Advertising

The Importance of Digital Advertising for Small Businesses

In today's digital age, the importance of digital advertising for small businesses cannot be overstated. With the vast majority of consumers turning to the internet to research products and services, it is essential for small businesses to have a strong online presence in order to compete in the market. Digital advertising offers small businesses the opportunity to reach a wider audience, increase brand awareness, and drive sales.

One of the key benefits of digital advertising is the ability to optimize your money for maximum results. By using targeted ads on social media platforms, small businesses can reach their ideal customers and maximize their return on investment. Social media platforms like Facebook, Instagram, and Twitter offer advanced targeting options that allow businesses to tailor their ads to specific demographics, interests, and behaviors, resulting in higher conversion rates and lower advertising costs.

In addition to social media advertising, small businesses can also benefit from optimizing their Google AdWords campaigns for maximum visibility. By carefully selecting keywords, targeting specific geographic locations, and optimizing ad copy, small businesses can increase their chances of appearing at the top of search engine results pages, driving more traffic to their website and increasing sales.

Another valuable tool in the digital advertising toolbox is retargeting ads, which allow businesses to target customers who have already visited their website or interacted with their ads. By showing these customers personalized ads based on their previous interactions, businesses can increase conversions and drive repeat business.

In order to fully optimize their digital advertising efforts, small businesses should also focus on optimizing their website content for improved search engine rankings. By conducting keyword research and creating high-quality, relevant content, businesses can improve their visibility in search engine results pages and attract more organic traffic.

Overall, digital advertising is a powerful tool for small businesses looking to increase their online visibility, attract more customers, and drive sales. By implementing targeted ads on social media platforms, optimizing Google AdWords campaigns, leveraging retargeting ads, and optimizing website content, small businesses can create a cohesive marketing strategy that delivers results. With the right strategies and tools in place, small businesses can maximize their online presence and achieve success in the digital marketplace.

Key Terms and Concepts in Digital Advertising

In the world of digital advertising, there are key terms and concepts that every small business owner should be familiar with in order to effectively optimize their online presence and maximize their ROI. Understanding these terms and concepts can help you navigate the complex landscape of digital advertising and make informed decisions about where to invest your advertising dollars.

One important concept to understand is how to optimize your money with digital advertising. This involves strategically allocating your budget across different advertising channels to reach your target audience effectively. By tracking and analyzing data from your campaigns, you can identify which channels are driving the best results and adjust your budget accordingly to maximize your ROI.

Another key concept is how to optimize your search engine for best traffic. This involves using targeted keywords and optimizing your website content to improve your search engine rankings. By conducting keyword research and implementing SEO best practices, you can increase your visibility in search engine results and drive more organic traffic to your website.

Using targeted ads on social media platforms is another important strategy for small business owners looking to maximize their ROI. By leveraging the advanced targeting options available on platforms like Facebook and Instagram, you can reach your ideal customers with tailored messaging that drives conversions. This targeted approach can help you get the most out of your advertising budget and see a higher return on investment.

In addition to social media advertising, small business owners should also consider optimizing their Google AdWords campaigns for maximum visibility. By carefully selecting keywords, writing compelling ad copy, and monitoring performance metrics, you can ensure that your ads are reaching the right audience at the right time. This targeted approach can help you drive more traffic to your website and increase your chances of converting leads into customers.

Overall, by understanding key terms and concepts in digital advertising, small business owners can create a cohesive marketing strategy that leverages the power of targeted advertising, search engine optimization, and data analysis to drive results. By implementing these strategies and staying informed about the latest trends in digital advertising, you can position your business for success in the competitive online marketplace.

Setting Goals and Budgets for Digital Advertising Campaigns

Setting goals and budgets for digital advertising campaigns is crucial for small business owners looking to optimize their money and achieve success in today's competitive online landscape. By establishing clear objectives and allocating resources effectively, businesses can maximize their return on investment and drive targeted traffic to their websites.

When setting goals for digital advertising campaigns, it is important to consider the specific outcomes you hope to achieve. Whether it's increasing website traffic, generating leads, or driving sales, having a clear understanding of your objectives will help you create focused and effective campaigns. By setting measurable goals, such as a target number of website visitors or a desired conversion rate, you can track your progress and make adjustments as needed to ensure success.

In addition to setting goals, small business owners must also establish realistic budgets for their digital advertising campaigns. Allocating the right amount of money to each campaign is essential for maximizing ROI and achieving your desired outcomes. By carefully planning your budget and considering factors such as targeting options, ad placements, and bidding strategies, you can optimize your spending and ensure that you are getting the most out of your advertising dollars.

One effective way to optimize your money with digital advertising is to use targeted ads on social media platforms. By leveraging the advanced targeting options available on platforms like Facebook, Instagram, and LinkedIn, businesses can reach their ideal customers with precision and maximize their return on investment. By tailoring your ads to specific demographics, interests, and behaviors, you can increase the likelihood of engaging with your target audience and driving conversions.

In addition to social media advertising, small business owners can also optimize their search engine visibility through strategies such as Google AdWords campaigns and retargeting ads. By focusing on relevant keywords, creating compelling ad copy, and optimizing landing pages for user engagement, businesses can improve their search engine rankings and drive more qualified traffic to their websites. By tracking and analyzing data from digital advertising campaigns, businesses can make informed decisions and continuously optimize their strategies for maximum effectiveness.

Optimizing Your Search Engine for Best Traffic

Understanding Search Engine Optimization (SEO)

Search Engine Optimization, or SEO, is a crucial aspect of digital advertising that every small business owner should be familiar with. SEO involves optimizing your website and online content to rank higher in search engine results pages, ultimately driving more organic traffic to your site. By understanding how search engines like Google rank websites and using the right strategies, you can significantly increase your online visibility and reach a larger audience.

One key aspect of SEO is using targeted keywords in your website content and meta tags. Keyword research tools can help you identify high-traffic keywords that are relevant to your business, allowing you to optimize your website for specific search terms. By incorporating these keywords strategically throughout your website, you can improve your chances of ranking higher in search engine results and attracting more visitors to your.

In addition to keyword optimization, creating high-quality, engaging content is essential for SEO success. Search engines prioritize websites that provide valuable and relevant information to users, so it's important to regularly update your website with fresh, compelling content. By publishing blog posts, articles, and other types of content that address the needs and interests of your target audience, you can improve your search engine rankings and establish your business as an authority in your industry.

Another important aspect of SEO is optimizing your website's technical elements, such as meta tags, URLs, and image alt text. These elements help search engines understand the content of your website and index it properly, making it easier for users to find your site when they search for relevant keywords. By paying attention to these technical details and ensuring that your website is structured and optimized for search engines, you can improve your site's visibility and attract more organic traffic.

Overall, SEO is a powerful tool for small business owners looking to maximize their online presence and reach a larger audience. By understanding the principles of SEO and implementing the right strategies, you can improve your search engine rankings, drive more organic traffic to your site, and ultimately increase your business's online visibility and success. By investing time and effort into optimizing your website for search engines, you can create a strong foundation for your digital advertising efforts and achieve long-term success in the competitive online marketplace.

Keyword Research and Analysis for SEO

Keyword research and analysis are essential components of any successful SEO strategy. By identifying the right keywords to target, small business owners can increase their visibility in search engine results and drive more traffic to their websites. Utilizing keyword research tools can help identify high-traffic keywords that potential customers are searching for, allowing businesses to tailor their content to meet the needs of their target audience.

In addition to conducting keyword research, small business owners can also leverage targeted ads on social media platforms to maximize their return on investment. By identifying their target audience and creating ads that resonate with them, businesses can increase their chances of reaching potential customers and driving conversions. Social media advertising allows businesses to reach a highly targeted audience, making it an effective way to increase brand awareness and drive sales.

When it comes to optimizing Google AdWords campaigns, small business owners can benefit from strategies that maximize visibility and drive traffic to their websites. By carefully selecting keywords, creating compelling ad copy, and optimizing landing pages for better user engagement, businesses can increase their chances of converting clicks into customers. Retargeting ads can also be used to increase conversions by targeting users who have previously visited a website, reminding them of products or services they may be interested in.

To improve search engine rankings, small business owners should focus on optimizing their website content with relevant keywords and creating a user-friendly experience for visitors. By regularly updating and optimizing website content, businesses can increase their chances of ranking higher in search engine results and attracting more organic traffic. Leveraging keyword research tools can help identify high-traffic keywords that can be incorporated into website content to improve visibility and drive more traffic.

By tracking and analyzing digital advertising and search engine data, small business owners can make informed decisions about their marketing strategies. A/B testing ads and landing pages can help optimize performance and improve conversion rates, while integrating digital advertising and SEO efforts can create a cohesive marketing strategy that maximizes visibility and drives traffic. By following these strategies, small business owners can increase their chances of success in the competitive digital advertising landscape.

Content Optimization for Improved Search Engine Rankings

In the world of digital advertising, one of the most important factors for small business success is optimizing your content for improved search engine rankings. By ensuring that your website and online ads are easily discoverable by search engines, you can increase your visibility and attract more traffic to your business.

To start, it's essential to understand the importance of using targeted ads on social media platforms to maximize ROI. By identifying your target audience and tailoring your ads to their interests and demographics, you can increase the likelihood of conversions and drive more traffic to your website.

Another key strategy for optimizing your digital advertising efforts is to focus on Google AdWords campaigns. By carefully selecting keywords, optimizing your ad copy, and monitoring performance metrics, you can ensure that your ads reach a larger audience and generate more clicks.

Retargeting ads are also a powerful tool for increasing conversions. By targeting users who have already visited your website or engaged with your ads, you can keep your brand top of mind and encourage them to take action.

In addition to optimizing your ads, it's crucial to pay attention to your website content. By incorporating high-traffic keywords, creating compelling ad copy, and optimizing your landing pages for better user engagement, you can improve your search engine rankings and attract more organic traffic to your site.

By leveraging keyword research tools, tracking and analyzing digital advertising data, and A/B testing your ads and landing pages, you can make informed decisions that drive better results. By integrating your digital advertising and SEO efforts, you can create a cohesive marketing strategy that maximizes your online presence and drives business growth.

Leveraging Targeted Ads on Social Media Platforms

Choosing the Right Social Media Platforms for Your Business

In today's digital age, having a strong presence on social media is crucial for small businesses looking to reach their target audience. However, with so many platforms available, it can be overwhelming to decide where to focus your efforts. Choosing the right social media platforms for your business is essential for maximizing your digital advertising budget and driving success.

When determining which social media platforms to invest in, it's important to consider your target audience and where they are most active. For example, if you are targeting a younger demographic, platforms like Instagram and TikTok may be more effective than Facebook or LinkedIn.

Understanding your audience's preferences and habits can help you narrow down the options and focus your resources where they will have the greatest impact.

Another important factor to consider when choosing social media platforms is the type of content you plan to share. Different platforms have different strengths and limitations when it comes to content formats, such as photos, videos, or text-based posts. For example, if your business relies heavily on visual content, platforms like

Instagram or Pinterest may be more suitable than Twitter or LinkedIn. Tailoring your content strategy to fit the platform can help you engage your audience and drive better results.

In addition to considering your target audience and content strategy, it's also important to evaluate the advertising options available on each platform. Some platforms, like Facebook and Instagram, offer robust targeting capabilities that allow you to reach specific demographics, interests, and behaviors. Others, like LinkedIn, may be better suited for B2B businesses looking to reach decision-makers in specific industries.

Understanding the advertising options and capabilities of each platform can help you maximize your return on investment and reach your business goals.

Ultimately, the key to choosing the right social media platforms for your business is to align your strategy with your goals and resources. By understanding your target audience, content strategy, and advertising options, you can make informed decisions that will help you optimize your digital advertising budget and drive success for your small business.

Remember, it's not about being on every platform – it's about being on the right platforms for your business.

Creating Targeted Ads for Different Audience Segments

Creating targeted ads for different audience segments is crucial for small business owners looking to maximize their return on investment in digital advertising. By tailoring your ads to specific groups of potential customers, you can increase the likelihood of attracting qualified leads and converting them into paying customers. In this section, we will explore various strategies for creating targeted ads that resonate with different audience segments and drive results for your small business.

One effective way to target different audience segments is by using social media platforms to deliver your ads. Social media platforms like Facebook, Instagram, and LinkedIn offer powerful targeting options that allow you to reach specific demographics, interests, and behaviors. By leveraging these targeting capabilities, you can ensure that your ads are seen by the right people at the right time, maximizing your return on investment and driving conversions.

Another key strategy for creating targeted ads is optimizing your Google AdWords campaigns for maximum visibility. By carefully selecting keywords, ad placements, and targeting options, you can ensure that your ads are shown to potential customers who are actively searching for products or services like yours. This targeted approach can help you attract high-quality leads and increase your chances of generating sales or inquiries.

In addition to targeting specific audience segments with your ads, it's also important to leverage retargeting ads to increase conversions. Retargeting allows you to show ads to people who have already visited your website or interacted with your brand, reminding them of your products or services and encouraging them to take action. By using retargeting ads strategically, you can increase conversions and maximize the effectiveness of your digital advertising efforts.

To further optimize your digital advertising and search engine efforts, it's essential to focus on optimizing your website content for improved search engine rankings. By using keyword research tools to identify high-traffic keywords and creating compelling ad copy that drives clicks and conversions, you can attract more traffic to your website and increase your chances of converting visitors into customers. Additionally, optimizing your landing pages for better user engagement and conversion rates can help you maximize the impact of your digital advertising campaigns.

By tracking and analyzing digital advertising and search engine data, you can make informed decisions about how to optimize your campaigns for better results. A/B testing ads and landing pages can help you identify which strategies are most effective and refine your approach to maximize your return on investment. By integrating your digital advertising and SEO efforts into a cohesive marketing strategy, you can create a more powerful and effective approach to reaching your target audience and driving business growth.

Analyzing and Adjusting Social Media Ad Campaigns for Maximum ROI

In the competitive world of digital advertising, small business owners must constantly analyze and adjust their social media ad campaigns to ensure maximum return on investment (ROI). This section will provide valuable insights and strategies for optimizing your money with digital advertising and search engine optimization to drive success for your small business.

One key aspect of maximizing ROI with social media ads is targeting the right audience. By leveraging the targeting options available on platforms like Facebook, Instagram, and LinkedIn, you can ensure that your ads are reaching the most relevant and engaged users. This targeted approach can lead to higher conversion rates and a better return on your advertising investment.

Another important strategy for optimizing social media ad campaigns is to track and analyze data on a regular basis. By monitoring key metrics such as click-through rates, conversion rates, and cost per acquisition, you can identify what is working well and what needs adjustment. This data-driven approach will help you make informed decisions about how to allocate your advertising budget for maximum impact.

In addition to social media ads, small business owners can also benefit from optimizing their Google AdWords campaigns for maximum visibility. By conducting keyword research, creating compelling ad copy, and optimizing landing pages for better user engagement, you can improve your chances of reaching potential customers when they are actively searching for your products or services.

Furthermore, retargeting ads can be a powerful tool for increasing conversions and maximizing ROI. By targeting users who have already shown interest in your business, you can stay top-of-mind and encourage them to take the next step in the purchasing process. By integrating digital advertising and SEO efforts, small business owners can create a cohesive marketing strategy that maximizes visibility, engagement, and conversion rates across all channels.

Maximizing Visibility with Google AdWords Campaigns

Setting Up and Managing Google AdWords Campaigns

Setting up and managing Google AdWords campaigns is essential for small business owners looking to optimize their money with digital advertising.

Google AdWords is a powerful tool that allows businesses to reach their target audience through targeted ads that appear in Google search results. By understanding how to effectively set up and manage AdWords campaigns, small business owners can maximize their return on investment and drive more traffic to their website.

One key strategy for small business owners looking to optimize their money with digital advertising is to use targeted ads on social media platforms to maximize ROI. Social media platforms like Facebook and Instagram offer highly targeted advertising options that allow businesses to reach their ideal customers. By creating ads that are tailored to specific demographics, interests, and behaviors, small business owners can increase their chances of converting leads into customers.

When it comes to Google AdWords campaigns, small business owners should focus on optimizing their campaigns for maximum visibility. This includes using relevant keywords, creating compelling ad copy, and optimizing landing pages for better user engagement. By constantly monitoring and tweaking their AdWords campaigns, small business owners can ensure that their ads are reaching the right audience and driving clicks and conversions.

Another important strategy for small business owners is to leverage retargeting ads to increase conversions. Retargeting ads allow businesses to target users who have previously visited their website but did not make a purchase. By showing these users relevant ads as they browse the web, businesses can increase their chances of converting them into customers.

In addition to managing Google AdWords campaigns, small business owners should also focus on optimizing their website content for improved search engine rankings. By using keyword research tools to identify high-traffic keywords and creating compelling ad copy that drives clicks and conversions, small business owners can improve their website's visibility in search engine results. By integrating digital advertising and SEO efforts, small business owners can create a cohesive marketing strategy that drives traffic and leads to their website.

Optimizing Ad Copy and Keywords for Better Performance

In the digital age, small business owners need to be strategic and efficient with their advertising efforts in order to compete in a crowded marketplace. One key aspect of maximizing your advertising budget is optimizing your ad copy and keywords for better performance. By fine-tuning your messaging and targeting the right keywords, you can increase your visibility and drive more traffic to your website.

When it comes to digital advertising, using targeted ads on social media platforms can be a game-changer for small businesses. By identifying your target audience and crafting ads that resonate with them, you can maximize your return on investment and see a higher conversion rate. Social media platforms like Facebook and Instagram offer robust targeting options that allow you to reach your ideal customers with precision.

Another important aspect of digital advertising is optimizing your Google AdWords campaigns for maximum visibility. By conducting keyword research and identifying high-traffic keywords, you can ensure that your ads are seen by the right people at the right time. By testing and refining your ad copy, you can drive clicks and conversions, ultimately increasing your ROI.

Retargeting ads are another powerful tool for small businesses looking to increase conversions. By targeting users who have already visited your website or engaged with your ads, you can remind them of your products or services and encourage them to take action. Retargeting ads can help you stay top-of-mind with potential customers and drive them further down the sales funnel.

In addition to optimizing your ad copy and keywords, it's important to focus on your website content and search engine optimization (SEO) efforts. By creating high-quality, relevant content that incorporates your target keywords, you can improve your search engine rankings and drive organic traffic to your site. By leveraging keyword research tools, you can identify the most effective keywords for your business and tailor your content accordingly.

Overall, optimizing your ad copy and keywords is essential for small businesses looking to make the most of their digital advertising budget. By targeting the right keywords, crafting compelling ad copy, and optimizing your website for search engines, you can increase your visibility, drive more traffic to your site, and ultimately, boost your bottom line. By implementing these strategies and tracking your results, you can make informed decisions and continuously optimize your digital advertising efforts for maximum effectiveness.

Monitoring and Analyzing Google AdWords Data for Insights

Monitoring and analyzing Google AdWords data is crucial for small business owners looking to optimize their digital advertising efforts. By keeping a close eye on key metrics such as click-through rates, conversion rates, and cost per click, you can gain valuable insights into the performance of your campaigns and make informed decisions to improve results.

One of the first steps in monitoring Google AdWords data is setting up conversion tracking. By tracking the actions that users take on your website after clicking on your ads, you can determine which campaigns are driving the most valuable leads and adjust your strategy accordingly. This data can also help you identify areas for improvement, such as optimizing landing pages or refining ad copy to increase conversions.

In addition to monitoring conversion metrics, it's important to analyze other key performance indicators such as quality score, impression share, and ad position. By understanding how these metrics impact your overall campaign performance, you can make strategic decisions to increase visibility and drive more targeted traffic to your website.

Another valuable tool for monitoring and analyzing Google AdWords data is the AdWords dashboard, which provides a comprehensive overview of your campaign performance in real-time. By regularly reviewing this data and identifying trends and patterns, you can identify opportunities for optimization and make adjustments to your campaigns to maximize ROI.

Overall, monitoring and analyzing Google AdWords data is essential for small business owners looking to optimize their digital advertising efforts. By leveraging key metrics, setting up conversion tracking, and utilizing tools such as the AdWords dashboard, you can gain valuable insights into your campaigns and make data-driven decisions to improve performance and drive business success.

Increasing Conversions with Retargeting Ads

Understanding Retargeting and Its Benefits

Retargeting is a powerful digital advertising strategy that allows businesses to target users who have previously interacted with their website or online content. By using cookies to track user behavior, businesses can show targeted ads to these users as they browse the internet, reminding them of products or services they have shown interest in. This form of advertising is highly effective because it reaches an audience that is already familiar with the brand, increasing the likelihood of conversion.

One of the key benefits of retargeting is its ability to increase conversions and ROI. By targeting users who have already shown interest in a product or service, businesses can significantly improve their chances of making a sale. Retargeting ads have been shown to have higher click-through rates and conversion rates compared to other forms of digital advertising, making them a valuable tool for small businesses looking to maximize their advertising budget.

In addition to increasing conversions, retargeting also helps businesses stay top-of-mind with potential customers. By showing targeted ads to users as they browse the internet, businesses can remind them of products or services they may have forgotten about or overlooked. This constant exposure can help drive repeat business and increase brand loyalty, ultimately leading to long-term success for the business.

When it comes to implementing a retargeting strategy, small business owners should consider using targeted ads on social media platforms to maximize ROI. Platforms like Facebook, Instagram, and Twitter offer robust targeting options that allow businesses to reach specific audiences based on demographics, interests, and online behavior. By creating compelling ad copy and targeting the right audience, businesses can increase their chances of converting users into customers.

Overall, retargeting is a valuable tool for small businesses looking to optimize their digital advertising efforts. By leveraging the power of retargeting ads, businesses can increase conversions, stay top-of-mind with potential customers, and ultimately drive more revenue. By understanding how retargeting works and implementing best practices, small business owners can take their advertising efforts to the next level and achieve greater success online.

Creating Effective Retargeting Campaigns

Retargeting is a powerful tool in digital advertising that allows small business owners to reach out to potential customers who have already shown interest in their products or services. By creating effective retargeting campaigns, businesses can increase their chances of converting leads into sales and ultimately maximize their return on investment.

One key strategy for creating successful retargeting campaigns is to use targeted ads on social media platforms to maximize ROI. By targeting specific demographics, interests, and behaviors, businesses can ensure that their ads are being seen by the right audience at the right time. This can help increase click-through rates and ultimately drive more conversions.

Another important aspect of creating effective retargeting campaigns is optimizing Google AdWords campaigns for maximum visibility. By using relevant keywords, ad extensions, and ad scheduling, businesses can increase their chances of appearing at the top of search engine results pages and reaching their target audience effectively.

In addition to using targeted ads on social media platforms and optimizing Google AdWords campaigns, businesses can also leverage retargeting ads to increase conversions. By showing ads to users who have already visited their website or interacted with their brand in some way, businesses can remind them of their products or services and encourage them to make a purchase.

To further enhance the effectiveness of retargeting campaigns, businesses should also focus on optimizing their website content for improved search engine rankings. By using high-traffic keywords, creating compelling ad copy, and optimizing landing pages for better user engagement, businesses can increase their visibility online and drive more traffic to their website.

Overall, creating effective retargeting campaigns requires a combination of targeted ads, optimized campaigns, and compelling content. By following these strategies and continuously tracking and analyzing data, small business owners can make informed decisions that will help them optimize their digital advertising efforts and maximize their success.

Analyzing Retargeting Data to Improve Conversions

In the digital age, small business owners have a plethora of tools at their disposal to optimize their advertising efforts and increase conversions. One key strategy that can have a significant impact on your bottom line is analyzing retargeting data. By understanding how your retargeting ads are performing, you can make informed decisions to improve your conversion rates and maximize your ROI.

One of the first steps in analyzing retargeting data is to track key metrics such as click-through rates, conversion rates, and cost per conversion. By monitoring these metrics, you can identify which ads are performing well and which ones may need to be adjusted or paused. This data can also help you understand the behavior of your target audience and tailor your messaging to better resonate with them.

Another important aspect of analyzing retargeting data is understanding the customer journey. By tracking how users interact with your ads and website, you can identify opportunities to re-engage with them and guide them towards conversion. For example, if a user visits your website but doesn't make a purchase, you can retarget them with a special offer or reminder to complete their transaction.

In addition to tracking key metrics and understanding the customer journey, small business owners should also leverage tools and technology to optimize their retargeting efforts. By using advanced targeting options, such as dynamic product ads or personalized messaging, you can create more relevant and engaging ads that drive higher conversions. Additionally, A/B testing different ad creatives and messaging can help you identify which strategies are most effective for your target audience.

Overall, analyzing retargeting data is a critical component of any successful digital advertising strategy. By tracking key metrics, understanding the customer journey, and leveraging advanced targeting options, small business owners can optimize their retargeting efforts to increase conversions and drive business growth. By taking a data-driven approach to your advertising efforts, you can make informed decisions that maximize your ROI and set your business up for success in the competitive digital landscape.

Creating Compelling Ad Copy and Landing Pages

Writing Engaging Ad Copy that Drives Clicks

In the competitive world of digital advertising, writing engaging ad copy that drives clicks is crucial for small business owners looking to optimize their money for success. Crafting compelling and persuasive ad copy is essential for attracting the attention of potential customers and driving them to take action. In this section, we will explore strategies and techniques for writing ad copy that resonates with your target audience and maximizes your ROI.

One effective way to drive clicks with your ad copy is to use targeted ads on social media platforms. By identifying your target audience and tailoring your messaging to their specific interests and needs, you can increase the likelihood of engagement and conversions. Social media platforms offer a wealth of targeting options, allowing you to reach the right people with the right message at the right time. By leveraging targeted ads on platforms like Facebook, Instagram, and LinkedIn, you can maximize your ROI and drive meaningful results for your small business.

Another important aspect of writing engaging ad copy is optimizing your Google AdWords campaigns for maximum visibility. By conducting keyword research and targeting high-traffic keywords, you can increase the chances of your ads being seen by potential customers. Additionally, creating compelling ad copy that highlights the unique value proposition of your products or services can help differentiate your business from competitors and drive clicks.

Retargeting ads are another powerful tool for increasing conversions and driving clicks. By targeting users who have already visited your website or interacted with your brand, you can re-engage them with personalized ads that encourage them to take action. Retargeting ads can be highly effective in driving conversions, as they target users who are already familiar with your brand and are more likely to convert.

In addition to writing engaging ad copy, it is important to optimize your website content for improved search engine rankings. By conducting keyword research and incorporating high-traffic keywords into your website content, you can increase your visibility in search engine results pages and attract more organic traffic. Optimizing your website content for SEO can help drive clicks and conversions, as users are more likely to click on websites that appear at the top of search results.

Overall, writing engaging ad copy that drives clicks is essential for small business owners looking to optimize their money with digital advertising. By using targeted ads on social media platforms, optimizing Google AdWords campaigns, leveraging retargeting ads, and optimizing website content for search engine rankings, you can increase your visibility and drive meaningful results for your small business. By following these strategies and techniques, you can create compelling ad copy that resonates with your target audience and drives clicks and conversions.

Designing Landing Pages for Better User Engagement

In the world of digital advertising, designing landing pages that engage users and drive conversions is crucial for small business success. A well- crafted landing page can make all the difference in turning website visitors into paying customers. In this section, we will explore the best practices for creating landing pages that captivate your audience and maximize your return on investment.

One key strategy for designing landing pages that engage users is to keep it simple and focused. Avoid overwhelming visitors with too much information or cluttered design elements. Instead, focus on a clear and concise message that guides users towards a specific action, such as making a purchase or signing up for a newsletter. By keeping your landing page clean and easy to navigate, you can increase user engagement and drive conversions.

Another important aspect of designing landing pages for better user engagement is to create a strong call-to-action. Your call-to-action should be clear, compelling, and prominently displayed on the page. Whether it's a button that prompts users to buy now or a form that encourages them to sign up for a free trial, your call-to-action should be the focal point of your landing page. By making it easy for users to take the next step, you can increase conversion rates and drive business growth.

In addition to a strong call-to-action, it's important to optimize your landing page for mobile users. With more people browsing the web on smartphones and tablets than ever before, it's essential that your landing page is responsive and mobile-friendly. By ensuring that your landing page looks great and functions smoothly on all devices, you can reach a wider audience and provide a better user experience.

Finally, tracking and analyzing data is essential for optimizing your landing pages for better user engagement. By monitoring metrics such as bounce rate, time on page, and conversion rate, you can identify areas for improvement and make data-driven decisions to enhance the performance of your landing pages. By continuously testing and refining your landing pages based on data insights, you can ensure that your digital advertising efforts are driving maximum results for your small business.

Testing and Optimizing Ad Copy and Landing Pages for Conversions

Testing and optimizing ad copy and landing pages for conversions is crucial for small business owners looking to maximize their return on investment in digital advertising. By continuously refining and improving their marketing materials, businesses can attract more qualified leads and increase their conversion rates.

One key strategy for optimizing ad copy and landing pages is to conduct A/B testing. This involves creating two versions of an ad or landing page with slight variations and testing them against each other to see which performs better. By comparing the results, small business owners can identify what resonates best with their target audience and make data-driven decisions to optimize their campaigns.

In addition to A/B testing, leveraging retargeting ads can also significantly increase conversions. By targeting users who have already shown interest in their products or services, businesses can stay top-of-mind and encourage them to complete a purchase. This personalized approach can lead to higher conversion rates and ultimately boost revenue.

Furthermore, small business owners can optimize their website content for improved search engine rankings by conducting keyword research. By identifying high-traffic keywords related to their industry, businesses can tailor their content to attract more organic traffic from search engines. This targeted approach can help improve visibility and drive more qualified leads to their website.

By utilizing these strategies and continuously analyzing data from their digital advertising and search engine campaigns, small business owners can make informed decisions to optimize their marketing efforts. By integrating digital advertising and SEO tactics, businesses can create a cohesive marketing strategy that maximizes their online visibility and drives conversions. Through testing and optimizing ad copy and landing pages, small business owners can effectively optimize their money for success in the digital advertising landscape.

Tracking and Analyzing Digital Advertising Data

Importance of Data Tracking and Analysis in Digital Advertising

In the world of digital advertising, data tracking and analysis are essential components for small business owners looking to maximize their marketing efforts. By carefully monitoring and interpreting key metrics, businesses can gain valuable insights into the effectiveness of their campaigns and make informed decisions to optimize their advertising strategies.

One of the main benefits of data tracking and analysis in digital advertising is the ability to measure ROI and determine the success of a campaign. By tracking metrics such as click-through rates, conversion rates, and cost per acquisition, businesses can assess the performance of their ads and make adjustments to improve results. This data-driven approach allows small business owners to allocate their advertising budget more effectively and focus on strategies that deliver the best return on investment.

Another important aspect of data tracking and analysis is the ability to target ads more effectively on social media platforms. By analyzing user behavior and demographics, businesses can create highly targeted ads that are more likely to resonate with their audience and drive conversions. This level of precision can help small business owners maximize their ROI and reach their ideal customers with the right message at the right time.

Furthermore, tracking and analyzing data can help businesses optimize their Google AdWords campaigns for maximum visibility. By monitoring keywords, ad performance, and competition, businesses can make strategic adjustments to improve their ad rank and increase traffic to their website.

This proactive approach to campaign management can help small business owners stay ahead of the competition and drive more qualified leads to their site.

In addition to optimizing ad campaigns, data tracking and analysis can also be used to leverage retargeting ads to increase conversions. By tracking user behavior and interactions with ads, businesses can retarget users who have shown interest in their products or services, leading to higher conversion rates and improved ROI. This personalized approach to advertising can help small business owners re-engage with potential customers and drive them further down the sales funnel.

Overall, data tracking and analysis are crucial tools for small business owners looking to succeed in the competitive world of digital advertising. By monitoring key metrics, targeting ads effectively, optimizing campaigns, and leveraging retargeting strategies, businesses can maximize their advertising efforts and achieve their marketing goals. With a data-driven approach to digital advertising, small business owners can make informed decisions, improve campaign performance, and ultimately drive more traffic, leads, and sales to their website.

Tools and Techniques for Analyzing Advertising Data

In the world of digital advertising, it is essential for small business owners to have a solid understanding of the tools and techniques available for analyzing advertising data. By utilizing these tools effectively, business owners can optimize their advertising budgets and improve their overall success in the digital landscape.

One key tool for analyzing advertising data is Google Analytics. This powerful platform allows business owners to track and analyze a wide range of metrics, such as website traffic, conversion rates, and user behavior. By leveraging Google Analytics, small business owners can gain valuable insights into the performance of their advertising campaigns and make data-driven decisions to optimize their strategies.

Another important tool for analyzing advertising data is social media analytics. Platforms like Facebook and Instagram offer robust analytics tools that allow business owners to track the performance of their targeted ads and measure their return on investment (ROI). By utilizing these tools, small business owners can refine their ad targeting strategies and maximize their advertising dollars on social media platforms.

In addition to using analytics tools, small business owners can also benefit from leveraging retargeting ads to increase conversions. Retargeting ads allow businesses to target users who have previously visited their website or engaged with their ads, increasing the likelihood of conversion. By incorporating retargeting ads into their advertising strategies, small business owners can boost their conversion rates and drive more sales.

To further optimize their advertising efforts, small business owners should also focus on optimizing their website content for improved search engine rankings. By incorporating high-traffic keywords and creating compelling ad copy, business owners can improve their visibility in search engine results and attract more targeted traffic to their websites. By using keyword research tools and implementing SEO best practices, small business owners can enhance their online presence and drive more organic traffic to their websites.

Overall, by utilizing a combination of tools and techniques for analyzing advertising data, small business owners can make informed decisions to optimize their advertising strategies and maximize their success in the digital landscape. By tracking and analyzing digital advertising and search engine data, conducting A/B testing, and integrating digital advertising and SEO efforts, business owners can create a cohesive marketing strategy that drives clicks, conversions, and ultimately, business growth.

Making Informed Decisions Based on Data Insights

In today's fast-paced digital world, small business owners must make informed decisions based on data insights to effectively optimize their digital advertising efforts. By leveraging the power of data, small business owners can maximize their return on investment and drive success in their online marketing campaigns. This section will explore various strategies and techniques for making informed decisions based on data insights, with a focus on optimizing digital advertising and search engine efforts for small business success.

One key aspect of making informed decisions based on data insights is understanding how to optimize your money with digital advertising.

Small business owners must carefully analyze their advertising budget and allocate funds strategically to maximize their ROI. By tracking and analyzing data from their digital advertising campaigns, small business owners can identify which strategies are most effective and make adjustments accordingly to optimize their spending for better results.

Another important aspect of making informed decisions based on data insights is optimizing search engine traffic. Small business owners must understand how to utilize targeted ads on social media platforms to maximize their visibility and reach their target audience effectively. By optimizing their Google AdWords campaigns and leveraging retargeting ads, small business owners can increase conversions and drive more traffic to their website.

Furthermore, small business owners must focus on optimizing their website content for improved search engine rankings. By using keyword research tools to identify high-traffic keywords and creating compelling ad copy that drives clicks and conversions, small business owners can improve their website's visibility and attract more potential customers. Additionally, optimizing landing pages for better user engagement and conversion rates is essential for maximizing the effectiveness of digital advertising efforts.

To make informed decisions based on data insights, small business owners must track and analyze digital advertising and search engine data effectively. By monitoring key performance metrics and using A/B testing to optimize ads and landing pages, small business owners can continuously improve their digital marketing strategies and drive better results. By integrating digital advertising and SEO efforts to create a cohesive marketing strategy, small business owners can maximize their online presence and achieve

long-term success in the competitive digital landscape.

A/B Testing for Optimal Performance

Understanding A/B Testing and Its Benefits

In the world of digital advertising, A/B testing is a powerful tool that can help small business owners optimize their marketing strategies for maximum success. A/B testing involves creating two versions of an ad or landing page, making a single change to one version, and then comparing the performance of the two to see which one yields better results. This process allows business owners to identify what resonates with their target audience and make data-driven decisions to improve their overall advertising efforts.

One of the key benefits of A/B testing is that it can help small business owners maximize their return on investment (ROI) by identifying the most effective messaging, design, and calls-to-action for their target audience. By testing different variations of ads and landing pages, business owners can ensure that they are putting their marketing budget towards strategies that are proven to drive results.

For small business owners looking to optimize their search engine traffic, A/B testing can be a game-changer. By testing different keywords, meta descriptions, and title tags, business owners can improve their website's visibility in search engine results pages and attract more organic traffic. This can help businesses increase their online presence, attract more potential customers, and ultimately drive more sales.

In addition to optimizing search engine traffic, A/B testing can also be used to maximize the effectiveness of targeted ads on social media platforms. By testing different ad copy, images, and targeting options, business owners can ensure that they are reaching the right audience with the right message at the right time. This can help businesses increase their return on ad spend and drive more conversions from their social media advertising efforts.

Overall, A/B testing is a valuable tool for small business owners who want to optimize their digital advertising and search engine strategies for success. By testing different variations of ads, landing pages, and keywords, business owners can identify what works best for their target audience and make data-driven decisions to improve their marketing efforts. By incorporating A/B testing into their overall marketing strategy, small business owners can drive more traffic, attract more customers, and ultimately grow their business online.

Implementing A/B Tests for Ads and Landing Pages

In the fast-paced world of digital advertising, small business owners need to constantly adapt and optimize their strategies to stay ahead of the competition. One powerful tool in their arsenal is A/B testing, which allows them to compare the performance of different ads and landing pages to determine which ones drive the best results. By implementing A/B tests for their digital campaigns, small business owners can make data-driven decisions that maximize their ROI and drive success.

When it comes to digital advertising, small business owners often struggle to identify the most effective ads and landing pages for their target audience. A/B testing provides a solution to this challenge by allowing them to test multiple variations of their creative assets and measure the impact on key performance metrics such as click-through rates and conversion rates. By running A/B tests on their ads and landing pages, small business owners can quickly identify which elements are resonating with their audience and make data-driven decisions to optimize their campaigns for success.

One key benefit of A/B testing for ads and landing pages is the ability to maximize ROI by focusing on what works best for the target audience. By testing different headlines, images, calls-to-action, and other elements, small business owners can identify the most effective combinations that drive the highest engagement and conversions. This allows them to allocate their budget more effectively and achieve better results from their digital advertising efforts.

In addition to optimizing ads and landing pages, A/B testing can also help small business owners improve their search engine rankings and drive more traffic to their website. By testing different keywords, meta descriptions, and other on-page elements, they can identify the most effective strategies for improving their visibility on search engine results pages. This can lead to increased organic traffic and better overall performance for their digital marketing efforts.

Overall, implementing A/B tests for ads and landing pages is a crucial step for small business owners looking to optimize their digital advertising strategies. By testing different elements and measuring the impact on key performance metrics, they can make data-driven decisions that drive success and maximize their ROI. By incorporating A/B testing into their overall marketing strategy, small business owners can stay ahead of the competition and achieve their goals in the digital landscape.

Interpreting Results and Making Data-Driven Decisions

As a small business owner looking to maximize your digital advertising efforts, it's crucial to interpret the results of your campaigns and make data- driven decisions to optimize your ROI. By understanding the data behind your ads and search engine optimization strategies, you can make informed choices that will help you reach your target audience more effectively.

One key aspect of interpreting results is analyzing the performance of your targeted ads on social media platforms. By tracking metrics such as click- through rates, engagement levels, and conversion rates, you can determine which ads are resonating with your audience and driving the most ROI. Use this data to refine your targeting and messaging to maximize your advertising dollars.

In addition to social media ads, optimizing Google AdWords campaigns is essential for maximizing visibility and driving traffic to your website. By analyzing data such as click-through rates, keyword performance, and conversion rates, you can identify opportunities to improve your ad copy, targeting, and bidding strategies. This data-driven approach will help you make informed decisions that will increase your ad's visibility and drive more traffic to your site.

Another powerful strategy for increasing conversions is leveraging retargeting ads. By analyzing data on user behavior and engagement with your website, you can create targeted ads that re-engage users who have previously visited your site but did not convert. This data-driven approach can help you increase conversions and drive more ROI from your digital advertising efforts.

To optimize your website for improved search engine rankings, it's important to analyze data on keyword performance and user engagement. By using keyword research tools to identify high-traffic keywords and creating compelling ad copy that drives clicks and conversions, you can improve your site's visibility in search engine results and attract more organic traffic.

By tracking and analyzing digital advertising and search engine data, you can make informed decisions that will help you optimize your campaigns for better performance. Strategies such as A/B testing ads and landing pages can help you identify what works best for your audience and make data- driven decisions to improve your ROI. By integrating your digital advertising and SEO efforts, you can create a cohesive marketing strategy that maximizes your online visibility and drives more traffic to your site.

Integrating Digital Advertising and SEO Efforts

Importance of Aligning Digital Advertising and SEO Strategies

In the digital age, having a strong online presence is crucial for small businesses looking to succeed in today's highly competitive market. One of the key components of a successful online marketing strategy is aligning digital advertising and SEO strategies. By ensuring that these two aspects work together seamlessly, small business owners can maximize their online visibility and reach their target audience effectively.

First and foremost, aligning digital advertising and SEO strategies helps small business owners optimize their marketing budget. By coordinating their efforts in these two areas, business owners can avoid wasting money on ineffective advertising campaigns or SEO tactics that don't drive traffic to their website. This ensures that every dollar spent on digital marketing is used efficiently and effectively, ultimately leading to a higher return on investment.

Furthermore, aligning digital advertising and SEO strategies allows small business owners to create a cohesive and consistent brand message across all online platforms. By using targeted ads on social media platforms to drive traffic to their website, optimizing Google AdWords campaigns for maximum visibility, and leveraging retargeting ads to increase conversions, business owners can ensure that their brand is consistently represented to their target audience.

In addition, aligning digital advertising and SEO strategies can help small business owners improve their search engine rankings. By optimizing website content with high-traffic keywords, creating compelling ad copy that drives clicks and conversions, and optimizing landing pages for better user engagement and conversion rates, business owners can increase their visibility in search engine results pages and attract more organic traffic to their website.

Lastly, aligning digital advertising and SEO strategies allows small business owners to track and analyze their digital marketing efforts more effectively. By integrating these two aspects of online marketing, business owners can make informed decisions based on data and analytics, A/B testing ads and landing pages to optimize performance, and ultimately create a cohesive marketing strategy that drives results and helps them achieve their business goals. By aligning digital advertising and SEO strategies, small business owners can maximize their online visibility, reach their target audience effectively, and drive results that lead to business success.

Creating a Cohesive Marketing Strategy

In the competitive world of digital advertising, creating a cohesive marketing strategy is essential for small businesses looking to optimize their money for success. By integrating various aspects of digital advertising, such as search engine optimization (SEO) and targeted ads on social media platforms, small business owners can maximize their return on investment (ROI) and reach their target audience effectively.

One key aspect of creating a cohesive marketing strategy is optimizing your search engine presence for the best traffic. This involves using targeted keywords, meta tags, and high-quality content to improve your website's visibility on search engine results pages. By implementing SEO best practices, small businesses can increase their organic traffic and attract more potential customers to their website.

Another important component of a cohesive marketing strategy is utilizing targeted ads on social media platforms to maximize ROI. By identifying and targeting specific demographics, interests, and behaviors, small businesses can reach their ideal customers and drive conversions. With the ability to track and analyze the performance of social media ads, small business owners can optimize their campaigns for maximum results.

Additionally, strategies for optimizing Google AdWords campaigns for maximum visibility are crucial for small businesses looking to increase their online presence. By selecting relevant keywords, creating compelling ad copy, and testing different ad variations, small business owners can improve their ad performance and drive more clicks and conversions.

Furthermore, leveraging retargeting ads can help small businesses increase conversions by targeting users who have already visited their website. By showing personalized ads to these users as they browse the web, businesses can stay top of mind and encourage them to make a purchase. Retargeting ads are a powerful tool for increasing conversion rates and maximizing ROI.

In conclusion, by integrating various digital advertising tactics, such as SEO, targeted social media ads, Google AdWords campaigns, retargeting ads, and website optimization, small business owners can create a cohesive marketing strategy that drives results. By tracking and analyzing data, testing different strategies, and integrating SEO efforts, small businesses can optimize their digital advertising efforts and achieve success online.

Maximizing Results by Combining Digital Advertising and SEO Tactics.

In today's digital age, small business owners must utilize a combination of digital advertising and SEO tactics to maximize their results and stay ahead of the competition. By integrating these two powerful tools, businesses can effectively reach their target audience, drive traffic to their website, and ultimately increase their ROI.

One key strategy for small business owners is to use targeted ads on social media platforms to maximize their return on investment. By identifying their target audience and tailoring their ads to their specific interests and demographics, businesses can ensure that their advertising dollars are being spent efficiently and effectively.

Another important tactic is to optimize Google AdWords campaigns for maximum visibility. By utilizing relevant keywords, ad extensions, and targeting options, businesses can ensure that their ads are appearing in front of the right audience at the right time, increasing the likelihood of clicks and conversions.

Retargeting ads are another powerful tool that small business owners can use to increase conversions. By targeting users who have already visited their website or shown interest in their products or services, businesses can remind them of their offerings and encourage them to make a purchase.

In addition to digital advertising, small business owners must also focus on optimizing their website content for improved search engine rankings. By conducting keyword research, creating high-quality content, and optimizing meta tags and descriptions, businesses can improve their visibility in search engine results and drive more organic traffic to their site.

By combining digital advertising and SEO tactics, small business owners can create a cohesive marketing strategy that maximizes their results and helps them achieve their business goals. By tracking and analyzing data, A/B testing ads and landing pages, and continuously optimizing their efforts, businesses can stay ahead of the curve and drive success in today's competitive digital landscape.

Navigating the Future with Emerging Digital Advertising Platforms

In the ever-evolving digital landscape, staying ahead means constantly seeking out new territories. Emerging digital advertising platforms offer untapped opportunities for small businesses aiming to carve out their niche in a crowded marketplace. This chapter delves into the promising realms of TikTok, Pinterest, Snapchat, and other burgeoning platforms, offering a roadmap for small businesses to navigate and thrive in these digital frontiers.

TikTok: Unleashing Creative Potential

TikTok has rapidly ascended as a powerhouse for creative content, particularly among younger demographics. Small businesses can harness TikTok by crafting authentic, engaging content that resonates with a vibrant community. Strategies for success include participating in trending challenges, collaborating with TikTok influencers, and utilizing TikTok Ads Manager to launch targeted campaigns that speak directly to desired audiences.

Pinterest: Pinning Your Way to Visibility

With its visually rich format, Pinterest serves as an ideal platform for businesses in design, fashion, home decor, and culinary arts. Pinterest ads, or Promoted Pins, blend seamlessly into the user's feed, offering a non-intrusive way to capture attention. Leveraging

Pinterest's unique search-driven user behavior involves optimizing Pin descriptions with keywords, creating inspirational boards, and employing Pinterest Analytics to refine strategies and boost engagement.

Snapchat: Capturing Moments, Capturing Audiences

Snapchat offers a unique proposition with its ephemeral content, appealing to a demographic that values spontaneity and privacy. Snap Ads, sponsored lenses, and geofilters provide innovative ways to engage users. Small businesses can capitalize on Snapchat's features by offering exclusive promotions, behind-the-scenes glimpses, and interactive content that encourages user participation and shares.

Navigating the New Frontier

Embarking on advertising in these emerging platforms necessitates a blend of creativity, strategy, and agility. Begin with a clear understanding of your target audience and which platform aligns with their preferences and behaviors. Test small-scale campaigns to gauge response and refine your approach based on performance analytics. Engage actively with your audience to foster community and brand loyalty.

Mastering Video Advertising Techniques for Small Business Success

In the digital age, video advertising stands as a cornerstone for small business marketing, offering a dynamic and compelling way to engage audiences. With its ability to convey messages quickly and memorably, video content has become indispensable in capturing the ever-shortening attention span of consumers. This chapter explores the art and science behind effective video advertising techniques, guiding small businesses through the creation and optimization of video content to enhance their digital presence and drive meaningful engagement.

Crafting Compelling Video Content

The foundation of successful video advertising lies in the creation of content that resonates with your audience. Begin with a clear understanding of your target demographic and the message you wish to convey. Storytelling is key; a well-told story can captivate an audience, evoke emotions, and foster a deeper connection with your brand. Consider the following elements:

- Engagement: The first few seconds of your video are crucial. Use eye-catching visuals and compelling narratives to grab attention immediately.

- Value: Your video should offer something of value – be it entertainment, information, or both. Videos that solve problems or address specific needs tend to perform better.

- Call to Action: Always conclude your video with a clear call to action. Whether it's visiting a website, signing up for a newsletter, or making a purchase, direct your viewers clearly on what to do next.

Optimizing Video for Different Platforms

Each social platform has its unique environment and user expectations. Tailoring your video content for each platform can significantly enhance its effectiveness:

- Facebook and Instagram: These platforms favor short, engaging videos that can capture attention even without sound. Consider adding subtitles and making your message clear with or without audio.

- YouTube: As a platform dedicated to video, YouTube allows for longer content, providing an opportunity to dive deeper into topics. Optimizing your video title, description, and tags with targeted keywords can also improve search visibility.

- TikTok: Creativity and trends reign supreme on TikTok. Short, catchy videos that leverage current trends or music can see significant engagement and shares.

Leveraging Video SEO

Search Engine Optimization (SEO) isn't just for text-based content; videos require optimization to ensure they are discoverable by search engines and potential viewers. Utilize keywords in your video title, description, and tags. Hosting your video on your own domain before uploading it to social platforms can also improve traffic to your website.

Measuring Success and Iteration

Effective video advertising is an iterative process. Utilize analytics tools provided by social platforms and Google Analytics to track the performance of your videos. Key metrics to monitor include view count, engagement rates, click-through rates, and conversion rates. Use these insights to refine your approach, test different content styles, and optimize your video marketing strategy.

Conclusion: The Power of Video Advertising

Video advertising offers small businesses a potent tool to tell their stories, connect with audiences, and drive engagement. By crafting compelling content, tailoring videos to various platforms, optimizing for SEO, and continuously measuring and refining your approach, your business can harness the power of video advertising to achieve remarkable success in the digital marketplace.

This section aims to empower small businesses with the knowledge and tools necessary to leverage video advertising effectively, enhancing their marketing strategy and fostering growth in an increasingly digital world.

Harnessing the Power of Influencer Marketing

In today's digital ecosystem, influencer marketing has emerged as a transformative strategy for small businesses aiming to expand their reach and connect with audiences in a more genuine and impactful way. Influencers — individuals with a substantial and engaged online following — can serve as powerful allies, lending their credibility and influence to promote your brand. This chapter will guide you through developing a successful influencer marketing strategy that aligns with your business goals and resonates with your target audience.

Understanding Influencer Marketing

At its core, influencer marketing is about partnership and storytelling. It involves collaborating with social media influencers to market your products or services. These influencers have the ability to affect the purchasing decisions of their followers because of their authority, knowledge, position, or relationship with their audience.

Identifying the Right Influencers

The first step in influencer marketing is identifying influencers who align with your brand's values, audience, and goals. Consider the following factors:

- Relevance: Choose influencers whose content aligns with your brand. Their followers should be your target customers.

- Reach: While the number of followers is important, focus on influencers who have a genuine connection with their audience.

- Engagement: High engagement rates often indicate an influencer's ability to effectively communicate with their audience.

Crafting Your Influencer Marketing Strategy

With the right influencers identified, it's time to craft a strategy that benefits both your brand and the influencers. Here are key components:

- Clear Objectives: Define what you hope to achieve with influencer marketing, whether it's increasing brand awareness, driving sales, or launching a new product.

- Authentic Partnerships: Work with influencers who are genuinely interested in your brand. Authentic endorsements resonate more with audiences.

- Creative Freedom: Allow influencers to create content that feels natural to their style. This authenticity is why their followers trust them.

- Measurable Goals: Set specific, measurable objectives for your campaigns. Use unique promo codes, affiliate links, or tracking URLs to measure performance.

Navigating Influencer Collaborations

Collaborating with influencers requires clear communication and mutual respect. Establish clear terms of the partnership, including expectations, deliverables, timelines, and compensation. It's essential to treat influencers as valued partners in your marketing strategy.

Measuring Success

Evaluating the effectiveness of your influencer marketing campaigns is crucial. Metrics to consider include:

- Engagement Rate: Likes, comments, and shares can indicate how compelling the influencer's content was.

- Traffic: Use tracking links to monitor the traffic influencers drive to your website.

- Conversion Rate: Track how many of those visitors convert into customers.

- Return on Investment (ROI): Assess the overall value generated from the campaign compared to the investment.

Building Success with Influencer Marketing

Influencer marketing offers small businesses a unique opportunity to reach their target audience through trusted voices in their community. By carefully selecting influencers, fostering authentic partnerships, and meticulously planning and measuring your campaigns, you can leverage influencer marketing to significantly boost your brand's visibility and credibility. As you embark on this journey, remember that the strength of influencer marketing lies in genuine connections and storytelling, making it a powerful tool in your digital marketing arsenal.

Navigating Privacy Regulations and Data Protection in Digital Advertising

In the digital age, where data is as valuable as currency, understanding and adhering to privacy regulations and data protection standards is crucial for small businesses. This chapter delves into the intricacies of navigating the complex landscape of privacy laws, providing small business owners with the knowledge needed to conduct digital advertising while respecting customer privacy and complying with global regulations.

The Importance of Privacy and Data Protection

With the advent of stringent privacy laws like the General Data Protection Regulation (GDPR) in Europe, the California Consumer

Privacy Act (CCPA), and others around the globe, the way businesses collect, store, and use consumer data has fundamentally changed. These regulations aim to protect consumers' personal information and afford them greater control over their data, imposing significant obligations on businesses.

Understanding Key Privacy Regulations

- GDPR: A regulation that requires businesses to protect the personal data and privacy of EU citizens for transactions that occur within EU member states.

- CCPA: Grants California residents new rights regarding their personal information, including the right to know, the right to delete, and the right to opt-out of the sale of personal data.

- Other Regional Laws: Many countries and regions have enacted or are planning to enact privacy laws. It's important to be aware of the regulations that apply to your business based on your geographical location and customer base.

Implementing Data Protection Practices

To comply with these regulations and protect your business from potential fines and reputational damage, consider the following practices:

- Data Minimization: Only collect data that is absolutely necessary for your operations and marketing efforts.

- Transparency: Clearly communicate to your users what data you are collecting, how it will be used, and how it will be protected.

- Consent: Implement mechanisms to obtain explicit consent from users before collecting their data. This consent should be freely given, specific, informed, and unambiguous.

- Data Security: Adopt robust security measures to protect stored data from unauthorized access, breaches, or theft. Regular security audits and updates can help in maintaining high security standards.

- Training and Awareness: Ensure that your team is aware of the importance of data protection and privacy laws. Regular training can help prevent accidental breaches or non-compliance.

Handling Data Breaches

Despite best efforts, data breaches can occur. It's vital to have a response plan in place, including:

- Immediate Action: Quickly secure your systems to prevent further data loss.

- Notification: Inform affected users and relevant authorities about the breach in accordance with legal requirements.

- Review and Improve: Analyze the breach to understand how it happened and implement measures to prevent future incidents.

Building Trust Through Compliance

In an era where consumer trust is paramount, adhering to privacy regulations and protecting data is not just a legal obligation but a competitive advantage. By implementing rigorous data protection strategies and respecting privacy laws, small businesses can build stronger relationships with their customers, enhance their reputation, and navigate the digital advertising landscape with confidence. Compliance with these regulations should be viewed not as a burden but as an opportunity to demonstrate your business's commitment to privacy and data protection.

Leveraging Advanced Analytics and AI for Strategic Digital Advertising

In the digital era, where competition is fierce and the pace of change is relentless, small businesses must leverage every technological advantage to optimize their advertising efforts and carve out a market share. Advanced analytics and Artificial Intelligence (AI) are at the forefront of this technological evolution, offering unprecedented insights and automation capabilities. This chapter explores how small businesses can harness the power of advanced analytics and AI to refine their digital advertising strategies, making them more effective and efficient.

The Power of Advanced Analytics

Advanced analytics involves the application of sophisticated analytical techniques to extract valuable information from data, helping businesses make informed decisions. Tools like Google Analytics provide a wealth of data on website traffic and user behavior, but advanced analytics goes further, offering deeper insights into customer patterns, predicting trends, and identifying opportunities for optimization.

AI-Driven Advertising

AI transforms digital advertising by automating complex processes, personalizing user experiences, and optimizing ad performance in real-time. Platforms like Facebook and Google use AI algorithms to automatically target ads, adjust bids, and manage ad placements, maximizing visibility and engagement.

Tools to Enhance Your Advertising Efforts

1. Google Analytics 4 (GA4): The latest iteration of Google's analytics tool, offering more comprehensive and granular data on user behavior, powered by machine learning to provide predictive insights and enhanced measurement capabilities.

2. AdRoll: Utilizes AI to automate ad campaigns across different platforms, optimizing ad spend by targeting users more likely to convert and providing detailed analytics to measure performance.

3. HubSpot: Offers a CRM platform that integrates AI and analytics to improve marketing strategies, providing tools for email marketing, social media management, and website analytics to enhance lead generation and customer engagement.

4. Salesforce Einstein: An AI layer within the Salesforce platform that offers predictive analytics, natural language processing, and automated data entry, helping businesses personalize customer interactions and predict future trends.

Implementing AI and Advanced Analytics in Your Strategy

To effectively implement AI and advanced analytics in your digital advertising strategy, consider the following steps:

- Data Collection and Management: Ensure that you have robust systems for collecting and managing data. Clean, well-organized data is the foundation of effective AI and analytics.

- Define Your Objectives: Clearly define what you want to achieve with AI and analytics, whether it's improving customer segmentation, personalizing advertising messages, or optimizing your advertising spend.

- Choose the Right Tools: Select tools and platforms that align with your objectives and integrate well with your existing systems. Consider factors like cost, scalability, and ease of use.

- Monitor and Iterate: Use the insights gained from advanced analytics and AI to continuously refine your advertising strategy. Monitor performance closely and be prepared to iterate and adapt based on what the data tells you.

Navigating the Future of Digital Advertising

The integration of advanced analytics and AI into digital advertising represents a significant shift towards more data-driven, efficient, and personalized marketing. For small businesses, embracing these technologies offers a way to level the playing field, allowing them to compete more effectively in the digital arena. By leveraging the right tools and adopting a strategic approach to analytics and AI, small businesses can unlock new opportunities for growth and innovation in their advertising efforts.

Mastering Interactive and Immersive Ads for Engaging Digital Experiences

In an era where consumer engagement is paramount, interactive and immersive advertisements stand out as innovative solutions that captivate and engage audiences on a deeper level. This chapter explores the transformative potential of interactive and immersive ads in digital advertising, offering small businesses a guide to harnessing these technologies to create compelling, memorable advertising experiences that drive engagement and conversions.

The Rise of Interactive and Immersive Advertising

Interactive ads invite users to engage directly with the content, whether through quizzes, polls, augmented reality (AR) experiences, or interactive videos. Immersive ads, particularly those leveraging virtual reality (VR) or AR, create an all-encompassing environment that deeply engages the senses, offering an unparalleled level of engagement. These ads not only capture attention but also foster a stronger emotional connection with the brand.

Benefits of Interactive and Immersive Ads

- Enhanced Engagement: By involving the audience directly, these ads boost engagement rates, keeping users interested and involved with your content longer.

- Increased Recall: The unique and engaging nature of interactive and immersive ads makes them more memorable, improving brand recall.

- Data Collection: These ads can provide valuable insights into user preferences and behaviors, informing future marketing strategies.

- Improved Conversion Rates: Engaged users are more likely to convert, making these ads an effective tool for driving sales and actions.

Implementing Interactive and Immersive Ads

1. Understand Your Audience: Tailor your interactive and immersive ads to the interests and behaviors of your target audience to maximize engagement.

2. Leverage the Right Technology: Utilize platforms and tools that support interactive and immersive ad creation, such as AR development platforms for AR ads or interactive video platforms for interactive storytelling.

3. Focus on Storytelling: Use these technologies to tell stories that resonate with your audience. Whether it's taking users on a virtual tour of your store with VR or using interactive quizzes to educate them about your products, storytelling is key.

4. Optimize for Mobile: With the majority of users accessing content on mobile devices, ensure your interactive and immersive ads are optimized for mobile viewing and interaction.

5. Measure and Optimize: Utilize analytics to measure the performance of your ads. Pay attention to engagement metrics, user feedback, and conversion rates to refine and optimize future campaigns.

Tools and Platforms for Creating Interactive and Immersive Ads

- Unity: A leading platform for creating immersive content, Unity is particularly powerful for developing AR and VR experiences.

- Wirewax or Eko: These platforms offer solutions for creating interactive videos that allow viewers to make choices that influence the narrative.

- Facebook AR Studio: Provides tools for creating AR experiences that integrate with Facebook's advertising platform, allowing for highly engaging social media campaigns.

Crafting the Future of Advertising

Interactive and immersive ads represent the next frontier in digital advertising, offering unparalleled opportunities for engagement, storytelling, and personalization. By embracing these innovative formats, small businesses can create advertising experiences that not only stand out but also forge deeper connections with their audience, driving both brand loyalty and conversions. As technology evolves, so too will the possibilities for interactive and immersive advertising, making it an exciting area for small businesses to explore and innovate within.

www.ingramcontent.com/pod-product-compliance
Lightning Source LLC
Chambersburg PA
CBHW070414230526
45471CB00006B/2804